The Immutable Fortress- Security in God's Unchanging Nature

Joshua Rhoades

Published by Joshua Paul Rhoades, 2024.

THE IMMUTABLE FORTRESS- SECURITY IN GOD'S UNCHANGING NATURE

First edition. August 26, 2024.

Copyright © 2024 Joshua Rhoades.

ISBN: 979-8227637666

Written by Joshua Rhoades.

Also by Joshua Rhoades

Courage Under Fire: David's Stand On The Battlefield

Jonah's Journey: Voices Of Redemption And Lessons In Obedience

The Furnace Of Faith: 12 Principles From The Heat Of Faith

Whispers of Hope: Inspiring Stories of Men's Prayers In Scripture

Frontier Legends: The Oregon Dream

Elijah: A Beacon Of Boldness

HOOK, LINE & SAVIOUR - Faith Reflections from Fishing

Driven By Faith: Motor Racing Inspired Christian Life

30 Day Devotional - Bold and Strong- Coffee Devotions for a Courageous Christian Walk

Authentic Christianity: The Heart of Old Time Religion

Consider The Ant - God's Tiny Preachers

Flee Fornication: The Plea For Purity

Renewed Hope- How to Find Encouragement in God

Sounding The Call - The Voice of Conviction

The Altar - Where Heaven Meets Earth

The Bible's Battlefields- Timeless Lessons from Ancient Wars

The Sacred Art of Silence - How Silence Speaks in Scripture

Under Fire- The Sanctity of the Traditional Biblical Home

Who Is on the Lord's Side? A Call to Righteousness

What Is Truth? - From Skepticism to Submission

The Immutable Fortress- Security in God's Unchanging Nature

Introduction

In a world that is constantly changing, where everything seems uncertain and unpredictable, the need for something solid and dependable is more important than ever. That's where God's unchanging nature comes in, like a fortress that cannot be shaken. The book, "The Immutable Fortress: Security in God's Unchanging Nature", invites readers to explore the comforting truth that, while everything around us may shift and change, God remains the same—yesterday, today, and forever. This book is about finding peace and security in knowing that God's character, promises, and love are unchangeable. When life gets hard, when we face challenges, or when we feel lost and unsure, we can find stability and hope in God's immutable nature. Just as a fortress provides protection and safety in the middle of a storm, God's unchanging nature offers us a safe place to stand, no matter what we are going through. Through stories, biblical truths, and practical applications, "The Immutable Fortress" shows us how to anchor our lives in God's unchanging character. It helps us understand that His promises are always trustworthy, His love is forever, and His power is constant. This book is a reminder that, no matter how much the world around us changes, we can always rely on God to be our rock and our refuge. In Him, we find the stability and security we need to face whatever comes our way, knowing that He is the same loving, just, and faithful God who has always been there for His people. So, if you've ever felt overwhelmed by the changes and uncertainties of life, this book will guide you to the unshakable truth that God is your fortress, and in Him, you can find true and lasting security.

Chapter 1 - God's Perpetual - Character

God's perpetual character is one of the most comforting and reassuring truths we can hold on to in life. In a world where everything seems to be constantly changing, where nothing stays the same for long, it can be easy to feel lost, confused, and even afraid. We face new challenges every day, from small inconveniences to life-altering events, and in the middle of all this change, it can sometimes feel like we have nowhere to turn. But the Bible gives us a powerful truth that we can anchor our lives to—a truth that brings peace, stability, and hope. This truth is found in Malachi 3:6, where God Himself says, "For I am the LORD, I change not; therefore ye sons of Jacob are not consumed." These words, though simple, carry a depth of meaning that can profoundly impact our lives.

Let's start by thinking about what it means for God to be unchanging, or, as the Bible puts it, immutable. The idea of immutability means that God's nature, character, and attributes are always the same. He doesn't change with the times or adjust His standards based on what is popular or acceptable in society. He is not influenced by external factors, nor does He need to evolve or improve because He is already perfect in every way. This is a concept that is hard for us to grasp fully because everything we know and experience in life is subject to change. Our feelings, our circumstances, the people around us—all of these things are constantly shifting. We grow older, we learn new things, we change our minds, and we adapt to new situations. But God is not like that. He is the same yesterday, today, and forever (Hebrews 13:8). This unchanging nature is what we refer to as God's perpetual character.

To better understand why this is so important, imagine you are in the middle of a storm at sea. The waves are crashing all around you, the wind is howling, and the boat you are in is being tossed about like a toy. It's a frightening experience, and you desperately look for something solid, something steady, to hold on to. In that moment, you see a lighthouse standing tall on the shore. No matter how fierce the storm gets, the lighthouse remains unmoved, shining its light to guide you safely to land. This is what God's perpetual character is like. He is that lighthouse, steady and unmovable, providing light and direction in the storms of life. No matter how chaotic things may get, we can look to Him and find safety and assurance.

But God's unchanging nature is not just about stability; it's also about His reliability and trustworthiness. Because God does not change, we can be confident that His promises are sure and His words are true. When He says something, He means it, and we can rely on it completely. This is a concept that brings a great deal of comfort, especially when we are going through difficult times. When everything around us feels uncertain, when the ground seems to be shifting beneath our feet, we can stand firm on the promises of God, knowing that they are as unchanging as He is.

Let's take a moment to reflect on what it would be like if God were not unchanging. If God were subject to change, then His promises could not be trusted. What He promised us yesterday might not hold true today, and we would have no assurance of His love or faithfulness. We would constantly be living in fear and uncertainty, never knowing if God's feelings toward us had changed or if His plans for us had been altered. This kind of uncertainty would be unbearable. But thanks be to God, we don't have to live with that fear. God's unchanging nature means that His love for us is eternal, His promises are secure, and His plans for us are good. This gives us a firm foundation to build our lives on.

In addition to reliability, God's immutability also means that His character is consistent. God is always good, always just, always loving, and always holy. These aspects of His character do not fluctuate based on the circumstances or on our behavior. For example, we might sometimes think that God is less pleased with us when we make mistakes or when we fail to live up to His standards. But God's love for us does not diminish when we fail. His love is based on His nature, not on our performance. This doesn't mean that God overlooks sin or that He is indifferent to our actions. On the contrary, because God is holy and just, He does care about how we live our lives. But His love for us is not conditional on our ability to be perfect. Instead, it is rooted in His unchanging nature.

Think about how reassuring this is. If God's love were conditional, we would always be worried about losing it. We would feel like we have to constantly earn His approval and that one wrong move could make Him turn away from us. But because God's love is based on His unchanging character, we can have confidence that His love is steadfast and enduring. This is the kind of love that we can rely on, no matter what. It's a love that gives us the courage to face our fears, to admit our mistakes, and to keep moving forward, knowing that God's love will never fail us.

God's unchanging nature also brings peace to our hearts. In the book of Isaiah, God says, "Thou wilt keep him in perfect peace, whose mind is stayed on thee: because he trusteth in thee" (Isaiah 26:3). This verse shows us that there is a direct connection between trusting in God's unchanging nature and experiencing peace in our lives. When we trust that God is who He says He is and that He will do what He has promised, we can rest in that assurance. We don't have to worry about what the future holds because we know that God is already there, and He is in control. This peace is not dependent on our circumstances. It is a peace that comes from knowing that, no matter what happens, God's character remains the same, and He is always working for our good.

Let's explore some practical ways we can apply this truth in our daily lives. One way to do this is by reminding ourselves of God's unchanging character whenever we face difficult situations. When we encounter challenges, it's easy to become overwhelmed by fear and doubt. We might start to question whether God is really in control or whether He really cares about us. But in those moments, we can choose to focus on the truth that God does not change. We can remind ourselves that He is the same God who has been faithful in the past, and He will continue to be faithful in the future. By focusing on God's unchanging nature, we can find the strength to face our challenges with confidence and peace.

Another way to apply this truth is by trusting in God's promises, even when it's hard to see how they will be fulfilled. Sometimes, life takes unexpected turns, and we find ourselves in situations that don't make sense. We might be going through a season of pain, loss, or uncertainty, and it can be difficult to see how God's promises will come to pass. But this is where faith comes in. Faith is not about seeing the outcome; it's about trusting in the One who holds the outcome in His hands. When we trust in God's unchanging nature, we can hold on to His promises, knowing that He is faithful to fulfill them, even when the path is unclear.

Another practical application of God's unchanging nature is in how we respond to the people around us. Because God's character is consistent, we are called to reflect that consistency in our own lives. This means being reliable, trustworthy, and faithful in our relationships. It means loving others with the same kind of steadfast love that God shows to us. It means being there for others in their time of need, just as God is always there for us. When we model our lives after God's unchanging character, we become a source of stability and strength for those around us.

This also impacts how we deal with our own failures and shortcomings. When we make mistakes, it's easy to feel like we've let God down and that He might be angry with us or disappointed in us. But remember, God's love for us does not change based on our performance. His love is constant, and He is always ready to forgive and restore us when we turn to Him. This doesn't give us a license to sin, but it does give us the freedom to admit our mistakes and seek God's forgiveness without fear of rejection. Knowing that God's love is unchanging gives us the courage to be honest about our struggles and to keep striving to live according to His will.

God's unchanging nature also gives us hope for the future. Because God is the same yesterday, today, and forever, we can be confident that

His plans for us are good and that He will continue to guide and protect us. We don't have to be afraid of what lies ahead because we know that God is already there, and He is in control. This gives us the freedom to live boldly and to pursue the dreams and goals that God has placed in our hearts, knowing that He is with us every step of the way.

One of the most beautiful aspects of God's unchanging nature is that it means His grace is always available to us. No matter how many times we fall, no matter how many mistakes we make, God's grace is always there to lift us up and set us back on the right path. His grace is not something that we have to earn or deserve; it is a gift that flows from His unchanging love for us. This grace is what empowers us to live the lives that God has called us to live. It gives us the strength to overcome our weaknesses, the courage to face our fears, and the hope to keep moving forward, even when the road is difficult.

Let's also consider how God's unchanging nature impacts our worship. When we come to God in worship, we are not worshiping a distant or unknowable deity. We are worshiping a God who is personal, loving, and unchanging. Our worship is a response to who God is and what He has done for us. Because God's character is consistent, our worship can be consistent as well. We don't have to worry about whether God is in a good mood or whether He will accept our worship. We can come to Him with confidence, knowing that He is always worthy of our praise and that He always receives our worship with love.

In addition, God's unchanging nature gives us the courage to stand firm in our faith, even when we face opposition. In a world that is constantly shifting and changing, it can be tempting to compromise our beliefs or to go along with the crowd. But when we remember that God does not change, we are reminded that His truth does not change either. We can stand firm in our faith, knowing that we are standing on the solid rock of God's unchanging word. This gives us the strength to hold on to our convictions, even when it's difficult or unpopular.

Finally, let's reflect on the impact of God's unchanging nature on our relationship with Him. Because God is unchanging, our relationship with Him is secure. We don't have to worry about God changing His mind about us or about His feelings toward us shifting. His love for us is steadfast, His promises are sure, and His presence is constant. This gives us the freedom to pursue a deep and meaningful relationship with God, knowing that He is always there, ready to meet us where we are. We can come to Him with all our fears, doubts, and struggles, knowing that He is always ready to listen, to comfort, and to guide us.

In conclusion, God's perpetual character is one of the most precious truths we can hold on to in life. It is a truth that brings stability, peace, and hope in a world that is constantly changing. God's unchanging nature means that His love for us is eternal, His promises are secure, and His plans for us are good. It means that we can trust Him completely, knowing that He is always dependable, always loving, and always there for us. As we go through life, we can find strength and courage in the knowledge that God is our immutable fortress—a refuge that will never fail us, a rock that will never be moved, and a source of light that will never dim. May we always place our trust in God's consistent character, knowing that in Him, we find true and lasting security.

Chapter 2 - God's Permanent Promises

God's permanent promises are like a fortress built on an unshakable foundation, providing us with a refuge of hope, strength, and unwavering security. In the book of Hebrews 6:17-18, we are reminded of the incredible truth that God, in His infinite wisdom and love, has made promises to us that are absolutely unchanging and forever reliable. The passage says, "Wherein God, willing more abundantly to shew unto the heirs of promise the immutability of his counsel, confirmed it by an oath: That by two immutable things, in which it was impossible for God to lie, we might have a strong consolation." These words carry a deep and profound significance for our lives because they tell us that God's promises are not just empty words or vague assurances. They are permanent, unchangeable, and absolutely trustworthy, giving us a strong foundation to stand on no matter what life throws our way. To truly understand the power of God's permanent promises, we must first consider the nature of promises in general. In our human experience, promises are often broken. People may make promises with good intentions, but due to changing circumstances, human weakness, or even dishonesty, those promises are not always kept. This can lead to feelings of disappointment, hurt, and mistrust. We have all experienced the pain of broken promises at some point in our lives, whether it's a friend who didn't keep their word, a family member who let us down, or even a personal goal that we failed to achieve. These experiences can make it difficult to trust anyone, and they can leave us feeling vulnerable and unsure of whom we can rely on. But when it comes to God, His promises are entirely different from those of humans. God is not limited by the constraints of time, circumstance, or human frailty. He is perfect, all-knowing, and all-powerful. When God makes a promise, it is not based on a guess or a hope that things will work out—it is based on His unchanging and perfect will. The passage in Hebrews tells us that God's counsel, His divine plan and purpose, is immutable, meaning it cannot change. When God makes a promise, He does so with full knowledge of the past, present, and future. He knows all things, and nothing can take Him by surprise. This means that when God promises something, He has already considered every possible outcome and has determined that His promise will be fulfilled. This truth should bring us immense comfort and confidence. Unlike human promises, which can falter and fail, God's promises are a sure thing. They are as solid and unchanging as God Himself. The passage also emphasizes that it is impossible for God to lie. This is a crucial point because it underscores the absolute reliability of God's word. When God speaks, His words are truth. There is no deception, no falsehood, and no hidden agenda. God's promises are pure and true, and they are given to us out of His boundless love and desire for our good. Because it is impossible for God to lie, we can have complete trust in everything He has promised. This is where the application of this truth becomes so powerful in our lives. Knowing that God's promises are permanent and unchanging allows us to persist in our reliance on them, no matter what challenges or uncertainties we face. Life is full of difficulties, and we often find ourselves in situations that test our faith and our resolve. There are times when we may feel overwhelmed, when our circumstances seem bleak, and when the future appears uncertain. In these moments, the temptation is to doubt, to question whether God's promises still hold true, or to wonder if He has forgotten us. But it is precisely in these moments that the permanence of God's promises becomes our anchor. When the storms of life rage around us, we can hold on to the promises of God with all our might, knowing that they will never change or fail. We can remind ourselves of His faithfulness throughout history, from the covenant He made with Abraham, to the deliverance of the Israelites, to the coming of Jesus Christ, who fulfilled the ultimate promise of salvation. Each of these examples shows us that God is a promise-keeper, and His word never returns void. In our own lives, we can look back and see how God has been faithful to His promises. Perhaps He has provided for us in times of need, given us peace in the midst of turmoil, or guided us when we were lost. These personal experiences are reminders that God's promises are not just abstract concepts—they are real, tangible, and active in our daily lives. And because God's promises are permanent, we can rely on them with absolute certainty, even when everything else is uncertain. For example, when we face financial struggles, we can trust in God's promise to provide for our needs (Philippians 4:19). When we are anxious or afraid, we can hold on to His promise to give us peace (John 14:27). When we are feeling alone or abandoned, we can find comfort in His promise to never leave us or forsake us (Deuteronomy 31:6). These promises are not just nice words to make us feel better—they are God's unchanging commitments to us, and they have the power to sustain us through even the most difficult circumstances. Another important aspect of God's permanent promises is that they are given to us as a form of assurance, a "strong consolation," as Hebrews puts it. This means that God's promises are meant to give us confidence and encouragement, especially when we are facing trials. In a world where so much is uncertain, God's promises are a source of unwavering hope. They remind us that we are not alone, that God is with us, and that He is working all things together for our good (Romans 8:28). This assurance is not just wishful thinking—it is based on the unchanging character of God and His proven track record of faithfulness. When we truly grasp the permanence of God's promises, it changes the way we live. It gives us the courage to step out in faith, knowing that God will fulfill what He has promised. It allows us to persevere through hardships, knowing that God's promises will ultimately come to pass. It fills us with a sense of peace, knowing that we are secure in God's hands and that His plans for us are good. In our relationships with others, the permanence of God's promises also inspires us to be promise-keepers ourselves. As we reflect on God's faithfulness, we are encouraged to be faithful in our own commitments, to keep our word, and to build trust with those around us. This is a powerful testimony to the reliability of God, as our actions reflect His unchanging nature to the world. In summary, the truth of God's permanent promises is a cornerstone of our faith. It is a truth that provides us with unshakable confidence, deep peace, and enduring hope. As we persist in our reliance on God's promises, we are reminded that they are immovable and trustworthy, just as God Himself is immovable and trustworthy. No matter what challenges we face, we can hold on to God's promises with the assurance that they will never change and that they will always be fulfilled. God's promises are a beacon of light in the darkness, a firm foundation in the shifting sands of life, and a source of unending comfort and strength. They are given to us by a God who loves us with an everlasting love and who is committed to our ultimate good. Let us, therefore, hold fast to God's promises, trusting in His unchanging nature and finding our security in the permanence of His word. In doing so, we will experience the fullness of God's peace, joy, and strength, and we will be able to face the future with unwavering hope, knowing that our God is faithful and His promises are forever.

Chapter 3 - God's Persistent Love

God's persistent love is like a never-ending river, flowing steadily and powerfully through every moment of our lives, no matter what we face or how we may feel. This love is beautifully captured in Jeremiah 31:3, where the Lord says, "Yea, I have loved thee with an everlasting love: therefore with lovingkindness have I drawn thee." These words reveal a truth that is both comforting and profound: God's love is not only persistent, but it is also everlasting. It is a love that has no beginning and no end, a love that is as constant as the rising sun and as unchanging as the stars in the sky. This love is a source of incredible comfort, especially in a world where so much is uncertain, and where human love can often fail or fade away. But God's love is different. It is a love that pursues us, that reaches out to us even when we are far away, and that holds us close no matter how far we may stray. It is a love that never gives up on us, that never grows tired or weary, and that never, ever stops.

To truly understand the depth of God's persistent love, we must first recognize that it is not like human love, which can be fickle and changeable. Human love is often conditional, based on feelings, circumstances, or how we behave. It can be influenced by many factors—how someone treats us, how they make us feel, or whether they meet our expectations. But God's love is not like that. It is unconditional, meaning it is not based on what we do or how we perform. God's love is rooted in His very nature, which is unchanging and eternal. This means that no matter what we do, no matter how many times we fail or fall short, God's love remains the same. It is persistent, always reaching out to us, always drawing us closer to Him with lovingkindness.

This truth is both humbling and empowering. It is humbling because it reminds us that we do not earn God's love—it is a gift that He freely gives us, not because we deserve it, but because He is a loving and gracious God. It is empowering because it means that we can rest in the assurance that God's love will never diminish. No matter what happens in our lives, no matter what mistakes we make, God's love will always be there, constant and unchanging. This is a truth that can bring incredible peace to our hearts. In times of trouble, when we feel alone, lost, or unworthy, we can remind ourselves that God's love is persistent. It does not waver or falter, and it is always reaching out to us, inviting us to come closer, to rest in His embrace, and to find our security and our identity in His love.

But God's persistent love is not just a passive force that waits for us to come to Him—it is active, always at work in our lives, even when we do not see or feel it. The verse in Jeremiah speaks of God drawing us with lovingkindness, which is a powerful image of how God's love pursues us. Even when we are unaware, God is at work, gently guiding us, calling us back to Him, and leading us toward His perfect plan for our lives. This is a love that does not give up, no matter how far we may stray or how often we turn away. It is a love that is always seeking us out, always desiring to bring us back into a close and intimate relationship with our Creator.

This persistent love of God is also incredibly patient. It does not rush or force its way into our lives, but waits for us to respond, giving us the freedom to choose. This patience reflects God's deep respect for our free will, but it is also a testament to His unwavering commitment to us. God's love is patient because He knows that true love cannot be forced—it must be freely given and received. This means that even when we resist, when we run from God, or when we make choices that lead us away from Him, His love remains the same. It is always there, waiting for us to turn back, to come home, and to receive the love that has been there all along.

One of the most beautiful aspects of God's persistent love is that it is personal. God's love is not a vague, abstract concept—it is specific and intimate. He knows each of us individually, with all our flaws, weaknesses, and struggles, and He loves us exactly as we are. This is a love that sees us fully, that understands us completely, and that loves us unconditionally. It is a love that is not based on our performance or our worthiness, but on God's unchanging nature. This personal love is what gives us the courage to be ourselves, to be honest about our struggles, and to come to God just as we are, knowing that we are loved and accepted.

God's persistent love also transforms us. When we truly grasp the depth of God's love for us, it changes us from the inside out. It gives us a new perspective on ourselves, on others, and on the world around us. It frees us from the need to earn love or approval from others because we know that we are already fully loved and accepted by God. This love empowers us to love others in the same way, with a love that is patient, kind, and forgiving. When we rest in the assurance of God's love, we are freed from fear and insecurity, and we are able to love others without holding back, without expecting anything in return, and without fear of rejection.

In practical terms, resting in God's persistent love means living each day with the confidence that we are loved and cherished by God. It means letting go of the need to prove ourselves, to earn approval, or to fear rejection. It means trusting that God's love is enough, that it is all we need, and that it will never fail us. This kind of trust allows us to live with a sense of peace and security, knowing that we are safe in God's hands, no matter what challenges or difficulties we may face.

Resting in God's love also means allowing His love to fuel our love for others. When we are secure in God's love, we are free to love others with the same kind of persistent, unconditional love that God has shown us. This means being patient with others, forgiving them when they hurt us, and loving them even when they do not deserve it. It means reaching out to those who are lost, hurting, or far from God, and showing them the same love that God has shown us. When we love others in this way, we become a reflection of God's love to the world, a living testimony of His persistent, unchanging, and everlasting love.

In summary, God's persistent love is a powerful and life-changing truth. It is a love that is everlasting, unchanging, and completely dependable. It is a love that pursues us, that draws us closer to God, and that transforms us from the inside out. It is a love that is personal, patient, and always present, no matter where we are or what we are going through. When we rest in the assurance of God's love, we find a deep sense of peace and security, knowing that we are loved and accepted by God, just as we are. This love gives us the courage to be ourselves, the strength to face life's challenges, and the freedom to love others with the same persistent, unconditional love that God has shown us. May we all learn to rest in God's persistent love, to let it fill our hearts and our lives, and to allow it to overflow into our relationships with others, so that the world may see and know the incredible love of our unchanging and everlasting God.

Chapter 4 - God's Perpetual Word

God's perpetual Word is like a mighty anchor in the vast and ever-changing ocean of life, providing us with stability, direction, and unwavering truth in a world that is constantly shifting and fading away. In Isaiah 40:8, we are reminded of a profound truth: "The grass withereth, the flower fadeth: but the word of our God shall stand for ever." This verse speaks to the eternal nature of God's Word, highlighting its enduring relevance and unchanging power throughout all generations. The grass and the flowers are beautiful, but they are temporary; they wither and fade with the passing of time, just as many things in life do. But in stark contrast, God's Word remains steadfast, unaltered, and forever applicable. This truth is a source of deep comfort and assurance, especially in a world where everything else seems so uncertain and fleeting. When we consider the temporary nature of so many things in our lives—our possessions, our achievements, our circumstances, even our own bodies—it can be easy to feel discouraged or anxious. But God's Word stands apart from all of this. It is not subject to the decay or change that everything else in our world is. Instead, it is eternal, unchanging, and perfectly reliable, offering us a solid foundation upon which we can build our lives.

To understand the significance of God's perpetual Word, we must first reflect on what it means for something to be perpetual. Perpetual means something that lasts forever, something that does not change with time, something that is eternal. When applied to God's Word, this means that the truths and promises found in Scripture are not just relevant for the time they were written but are applicable for all people, in all places, and in all times. God's Word does not become outdated or irrelevant, no matter how much the world changes. The wisdom, guidance, and truths found in the Bible are as applicable today as they were thousands of years ago. This is a powerful and reassuring thought because it means that no matter what we face in life, we can always turn to God's Word for guidance, comfort, and truth.

In a world where trends, opinions, and even laws are constantly changing, having something unchanging and reliable to hold onto is incredibly valuable. Many people build their lives around things that are temporary—careers, relationships, material possessions, or societal trends. But when these things fade away or fail to fulfill us, it can leave us feeling lost and without direction. God's Word, however, offers us a foundation that will never crumble. It provides us with timeless truths that can guide us through every situation we encounter, no matter how much the world around us changes. The wisdom of Scripture is not bound by the limitations of time or culture; it transcends all of that, offering us guidance and truth that are always relevant, no matter where we are or what we are going through.

One of the most remarkable aspects of God's Word is its ability to speak into every area of our lives. Whether we are dealing with personal struggles, relationship issues, questions about our purpose, or the challenges of living in a complex and often confusing world, the Bible has something to say. Its teachings provide us with the principles and values that help us navigate life's challenges with wisdom and grace. The Bible is not just a book of ancient stories or moral teachings; it is a living, breathing Word from God that continues to speak to us today. It is full of practical wisdom, profound truths, and timeless guidance that help us live lives that are pleasing to God and fulfilling for us.

For example, when we face uncertainty or fear about the future, God's Word reassures us that He is in control and that He has good plans for our lives (Jeremiah 29:11). When we feel burdened by guilt or shame, Scripture reminds us of God's forgiveness and grace (1 John 1:9). When we are confused about what to do or which path to take, the Bible provides us with guidance and direction (Proverbs 3:5-6). These truths are not just comforting; they are also empowering because they give us the confidence to face whatever comes our way, knowing that we have a solid foundation to stand on.

Building our lives on the unchanging truth of Scripture also means allowing God's Word to shape our values, our decisions, and our actions. It means prioritizing God's truth over the shifting opinions and trends of the world. In a culture that often values success, wealth, and power, the Bible calls us to a different way of living—one that is centered on love, humility, and service to others. It challenges us to think differently, to act differently, and to live lives that reflect the values of God's Kingdom rather than the values of the world. This can be difficult, especially when the world around us seems to be moving in a different direction. But when we build our lives on the unchanging truth of Scripture, we find that we are not swayed by the shifting tides of culture or opinion. Instead, we are anchored in God's truth, which provides us with the wisdom and guidance we need to navigate life's challenges with integrity and grace.

Another important aspect of building our lives on God's Word is the importance of consistently engaging with Scripture. The Bible is not just a book to be read once and then put aside; it is meant to be a daily source of inspiration, guidance, and encouragement. As we read and meditate on God's Word, we allow it to shape our thoughts, our attitudes, and our actions. We begin to see the world through the lens of Scripture, which helps us to make decisions that align with God's will and purpose for our lives. This process of engaging with God's Word is not just about gaining knowledge; it is about allowing God's truth to transform us from the inside out.

The perpetual nature of God's Word also means that it is a reliable source of truth in a world where truth is often seen as relative or subjective. Many people today believe that truth is something that can change based on personal beliefs, cultural trends, or societal norms. But the Bible teaches us that truth is absolute and unchanging. God's Word is the standard by which all other truth is measured. It provides us with a clear understanding of who God is, who we are, and how we are to live our lives. This truth is not just theoretical; it is practical and applicable to every aspect of our lives. It gives us the clarity and direction we need to make wise decisions, to build healthy relationships, and to live lives that are pleasing to God.

Furthermore, the eternal nature of God's Word means that it is relevant for all people, in all places, and at all times. The truths found in Scripture are not limited to a specific time period or cultural context; they are universal and timeless. This means that no matter where we live, what language we speak, or what culture we are a part of, God's Word has something to say to us. It speaks to the deepest needs of the human heart, offering hope, healing, and guidance. It addresses the universal struggles and challenges that we all face—fear, doubt, loneliness, pain, and the search for meaning and purpose. And it offers us the answers we are looking for, pointing us to the God who created us, who loves us, and who has a plan for our lives.

One of the most powerful ways that God's Word impacts our lives is through the promises it contains. The Bible is full of promises from God—promises of His love, His presence, His provision, His protection, and His guidance. These promises are not just empty words; they are backed by the unchanging character of God. When God makes a promise, we can be sure that He will fulfill it. This gives us incredible confidence and hope, even in the midst of difficult circumstances. When we are going through a tough time, we can hold on to God's promises, knowing that He is faithful and that His Word is true. This is why it is so important to know God's Word and to meditate on His promises. When we fill our hearts and minds with the truth of Scripture, we are equipped to face whatever challenges come our way with faith and confidence.

The perpetual nature of God's Word also means that it is a source of ongoing revelation. As we continue to study and meditate on Scripture, God reveals new insights and truths to us. This is one of the reasons why the Bible is often described as a living book. It is not static or outdated; it is alive with the power of God's Spirit, continually speaking to us and guiding us into deeper understanding and relationship with Him. No matter how many times we read a passage or a verse, there is always more to discover, more to learn, and more ways to apply God's truth to our lives. This ongoing revelation is one of the ways that God's Word remains relevant and applicable to us throughout our lives.

In conclusion, God's perpetual Word is an unchanging and reliable source of truth, wisdom, and guidance in a world that is constantly changing. It is a solid foundation upon which we can build our lives, offering us stability, direction, and hope. The truths and promises found in Scripture are timeless and universal, applicable to every aspect of our lives, no matter where we are or what we are going through. As we prioritize building our lives on the unchanging truth of God's Word, we are equipped to navigate life's challenges with wisdom, grace, and confidence. We are anchored in a truth that does not change, that does not fade, and that will stand forever. May we always seek to know and live by God's Word, trusting in its perpetual relevance and power to guide us, to comfort us, and to transform us.

Chapter 5 - God's Preserved Covenant

God's preserved covenant is like a sacred, unbreakable bond that binds us to Him in a relationship of unwavering love, faithfulness, and commitment, a bond that is secure and eternal because it is founded on God's unchanging nature. In Psalm 89:34, God declares, "My covenant will I not break, nor alter the thing that is gone out of my lips." This profound truth reveals the heart of God's faithfulness and the depth of His commitment to His promises. Unlike human agreements that can be broken, altered, or forgotten, God's covenant stands firm and immovable throughout all time. It is preserved in the purity of His word, untainted by time or circumstance, and it remains as reliable today as it was when He first made it. The word "covenant" itself speaks of a solemn agreement, a promise made with the deepest sincerity and commitment, often sealed with a sacred act. In the Bible, covenants represent God's enduring promises to His people—promises that are not based on human merit or performance, but on His steadfast character and everlasting love. The covenant is a testament to God's desire to be in a relationship with us, a relationship that is not subject to the whims of change or the failures of human nature, but one that is grounded in the very essence of who God is: faithful, true, and unchanging.

To fully appreciate the significance of God's preserved covenant, we must first understand the nature of a covenant in the biblical sense. A covenant in the Bible is not just a contract or an agreement between two parties; it is a binding promise that involves a deep, personal commitment. It is an agreement that God initiates, and it is marked by His absolute faithfulness. Throughout the Bible, we see God making covenants with His people—promises that He keeps no matter what. He made a covenant with Noah, promising never to destroy the earth with a flood again, and sealed that promise with the sign of a rainbow. He made a covenant with Abraham, promising to make him the father of many nations, and that covenant was marked by the sign of circumcision.

He made a covenant with the Israelites at Mount Sinai, giving them the Law and promising to be their God if they would be His people. And ultimately, He made a new covenant through Jesus Christ, promising eternal life to all who believe in Him, sealed by the blood of Christ.

Each of these covenants is a reflection of God's unchanging nature and His desire to be in a relationship with us. They show us that God is not just interested in making promises; He is committed to keeping them, no matter the cost. This is what makes His covenant preserved and unbreakable. God's covenant is not like a human contract that can be voided or renegotiated; it is a sacred bond that He will never break or alter. His words, once spoken, are eternal and trustworthy, because they are backed by His immutable character. When God says, "My covenant will I not break," He is assuring us that His promises are secure, that they are not subject to change or cancellation. This is a powerful truth that brings immense comfort and security to our hearts. It means that no matter what happens in our lives, no matter how we may falter or fail, God's promises to us remain intact. His commitment to us does not waver, and His love for us does not diminish.

This preserved covenant is a foundation upon which we can build our lives. It is a source of unshakable confidence, knowing that our relationship with God is not based on our ability to keep our end of the bargain, but on His faithfulness to keep His promises. In a world where so many things are uncertain and changeable, God's covenant is a rock-solid foundation. It is something we can rely on completely, knowing that it will never be broken. This truth frees us from the fear of abandonment or rejection because we know that God's commitment to us is eternal. His covenant is a testament to His unchanging nature, and it gives us the assurance that we are always secure in His love.

One of the most profound implications of God's preserved covenant is that it is entirely rooted in His grace. The covenants God makes are not based on what we do or how well we perform; they are based on His grace and His desire to bless us and be in a relationship with us.

This means that even when we fall short, even when we make mistakes, God's covenant remains. It is not dependent on our actions, but on His character. This is a truth that brings incredible peace and relief, knowing that our standing with God is not something we have to earn or maintain by our efforts, but something that is given to us freely because of who God is. His covenant is a gift of grace, one that we can receive with open hearts and thankful spirits.

God's preserved covenant also reveals His desire for a deep and lasting relationship with us. The fact that God makes covenants with His people shows us that He is not distant or detached; He is intimately involved in our lives and deeply committed to us. He wants us to know Him, to trust Him, and to live in a relationship with Him that is marked by love, faithfulness, and trust. This relationship is not a casual or temporary one; it is eternal and unbreakable, founded on God's unchanging promises. It is a relationship that God Himself initiates and sustains, one that He invites us into with open arms.

Living in light of God's preserved covenant means putting our confidence in the relationship we have with Him. It means trusting that His promises are true and that His commitment to us is unwavering. It means living with the assurance that God is for us, that He is always faithful, and that He will never leave us or forsake us. This confidence changes the way we live. It gives us the courage to face challenges, knowing that God is with us and that His promises will never fail. It gives us the peace to rest in His love, knowing that our relationship with Him is secure. And it gives us the hope to keep moving forward, even when life is difficult, because we know that God's covenant is preserved and unbreakable.

In practical terms, living in the assurance of God's preserved covenant means turning to Him in every situation, trusting that His promises are true. It means holding on to His Word, even when circumstances seem to contradict it. It means remembering that God's covenant is not based on our performance but on His grace, and allowing that truth to fill us with peace and confidence. It means living with a deep sense of security, knowing that we are loved by a God who is faithful, who keeps His promises, and who will never break His covenant with us.

This truth also inspires us to be faithful in our own relationships. As we reflect on God's faithfulness to His covenant, we are called to be faithful in our commitments to others. Whether in our marriages, our friendships, or our community, we are called to reflect the faithfulness of God in the way we love, serve, and support those around us. This is a powerful testimony to the world of God's unchanging nature, as we live out the truth of His preserved covenant in our daily lives.

In summary, God's preserved covenant is a profound and powerful truth that offers us deep comfort, security, and confidence. It is a testament to God's unchanging nature and His unwavering commitment to His promises. It is a relationship that is not based on our performance but on His grace, and it is a relationship that is eternal and unbreakable. As we live in the assurance of God's preserved covenant, we are freed from fear and insecurity, and we are empowered to live lives of faith, trust, and love. We are called to put our confidence in the covenant relationship we have with God, assured that it is securely founded on His immutability. May we always hold fast to the truth of God's preserved covenant, trusting in His faithfulness, and living in the security and peace that come from knowing that His promises are forever unbroken and His love for us is eternal.

Chapter 6 - God's Persistent Faithfulness

God's persistent faithfulness is like a warm, unending embrace that holds us steady through every storm and every trial we face in life, a steadfast presence that never wavers, never weakens, and never fails us, no matter how dark the night or how difficult the journey. In Lamentations 3:22-23, the Bible reminds us of this profound truth: "It is of the LORD'S mercies that we are not consumed, because his compassions fail not. They are new every morning: great is thy faithfulness." These words, spoken in the midst of immense suffering and sorrow, shine like a beacon of hope, revealing the depth and constancy of God's love and mercy toward us. His faithfulness is not just a passive quality; it is active, persistent, and unfailing, a relentless commitment to care for us, to provide for us, and to sustain us through all of life's ups and downs. This faithfulness is the very heartbeat of our relationship with God, the solid ground beneath our feet when everything else seems to be crumbling. It is because of His great faithfulness that we are not consumed, that we are not overwhelmed by the weight of our burdens, or crushed by the trials we endure. Every morning, as the sun rises, God's faithfulness is renewed, offering us fresh mercies and new strength to face the day ahead. It is a faithfulness that is not dependent on our actions or our worthiness, but on God's unchanging character and His boundless love for us.

To truly grasp the power and significance of God's persistent faithfulness, we must first understand what it means for God to be faithful. Faithfulness, in its simplest form, is about keeping promises, being reliable, and remaining true to one's word. But when we talk about God's faithfulness, we are speaking of something far deeper and more profound than human faithfulness. God's faithfulness is absolute and perfect; it is a reflection of His very nature. Unlike humans, who can be unfaithful, inconsistent, and unreliable, God is always faithful. He never breaks a promise, never forgets His word, and never abandons His people. His faithfulness is rooted in His unchanging nature, which means it is as steadfast as He is. No matter how much we change, no matter how often we fail or fall short, God remains faithful. He does not waver in His commitment to us, and He does not withhold His mercy or compassion from us, even when we least deserve it.

This truth is both comforting and humbling. It is comforting because it means that we can always rely on God, no matter what we are going through. When life is hard, when we are facing challenges that seem insurmountable, when we feel lost, alone, or afraid, we can turn to God and know that He is there, that He is faithful, and that He will not let us down. His faithfulness is a constant in our lives, something we can depend on when everything else is uncertain. It is a rock we can cling to in the storm, a refuge we can run to when we are in trouble. But this truth is also humbling because it reminds us that we are not in control, that we are not self-sufficient, and that we cannot make it on our own. We need God's faithfulness; we need His mercy and His compassion every single day. Without them, we would be consumed, overwhelmed by the weight of our own sin, our own failures, and the trials of life. But because God is faithful, because His mercies are new every morning, we are sustained, we are strengthened, and we are given the grace we need to keep going.

One of the most beautiful aspects of God's faithfulness is that it is persistent. It does not give up on us, even when we give up on ourselves. It is a faithfulness that pursues us, that reaches out to us in our darkest moments, and that holds us close when we feel like we are falling apart. God's faithfulness is like a gentle hand that lifts us up when we are down, like a steady voice that reassures us when we are afraid, like a strong arm that supports us when we are weak. It is a faithfulness that meets us where we are, no matter how far we have strayed, no matter how broken we feel, and no matter how lost we seem. God's faithfulness is a reminder that we are never alone, that we are never beyond the reach of His love, and that we are always in His care.

Living in the light of God's persistent faithfulness means trusting Him in every situation, no matter how difficult or overwhelming it may seem. It means believing that God is who He says He is, that He will do what He has promised, and that He will never leave us or forsake us. This kind of trust is not always easy, especially when we are faced with circumstances that challenge our faith or shake our confidence. But it is in these moments that God's faithfulness shines the brightest. When we are weak, He is strong. When we are fearful, He is our peace. When we are lost, He is our guide. God's faithfulness is a constant reminder that we can depend on Him, that we can lean on Him, and that we can find rest in His unchanging love.

In practical terms, depending on God's faithfulness means turning to Him in prayer, seeking His guidance in His Word, and trusting His timing and His plan for our lives. It means letting go of our need to control everything and allowing God to be in control. It means acknowledging that we cannot do it all on our own, that we need His help, His strength, and His grace to get through each day. And it means resting in the assurance that no matter what happens, God is faithful, and He will see us through. This kind of dependence is not a sign of weakness, but of wisdom. It is recognizing that true strength comes from relying on God, not on ourselves, and that true peace comes from trusting in His faithfulness, not in our own abilities.

God's persistent faithfulness also calls us to be faithful in return. As we experience God's unwavering commitment to us, we are called to respond with faithfulness in our own lives. This means being faithful in our relationships, faithful in our responsibilities, and faithful in our walk with God. It means keeping our promises, standing by our commitments, and living with integrity and honesty. It means being reliable, dependable, and trustworthy, just as God is with us. But even as we strive to be faithful, we know that we will never be perfect. We will stumble, we will fail, and we will fall short. But even then, God's faithfulness does not waver. He is always there to pick us up, to forgive us, and to help us start again. His faithfulness is the foundation that allows us to keep going, to keep trying, and to keep growing in our relationship with Him.

One of the most powerful ways that God's faithfulness impacts our lives is through the way it shapes our understanding of who He is. When we see God's faithfulness in action—when we experience His mercy, His compassion, and His care for us—it changes the way we see Him. We begin to understand that God is not distant or detached, but deeply involved in our lives. We see that He is not just a God of rules and commandments, but a God of love, grace, and faithfulness. This understanding transforms our relationship with Him, making it more intimate, more personal, and more real. We begin to trust Him more, to rely on Him more, and to love Him more deeply. And as our relationship with God grows, so does our faith, our hope, and our joy.

In conclusion, God's persistent faithfulness is a truth that anchors our souls, that gives us hope in the darkest of times, and that sustains us through every challenge we face. It is a faithfulness that is unfailing, unchanging, and unwavering, rooted in God's perfect character and His boundless love for us. As we live in the light of God's faithfulness, we are called to trust Him in every situation, to depend on Him in every trial, and to rest in the assurance that He is always with us. His faithfulness is a constant reminder that we are not alone, that we are deeply loved, and that we are always in His care. May we persist in depending on God's unwavering faithfulness, knowing that He is always reliable, always present, and always faithful to His promises. In doing so, we will find the strength to face each day with confidence, the peace to rest in His love, and the joy to live fully in His grace.

Chapter 7 - God's Predestined Purpose

God's predestined purpose is like a masterful, unchangeable plan that guides our lives with precision and wisdom, a divine blueprint that was crafted with love and intention long before we took our first breath. In Proverbs 19:21, the Bible tells us, "There are many devices in a man's heart; nevertheless the counsel of the LORD, that shall stand." This verse captures a profound truth about our lives and the world we live in: while we may have our own plans, desires, and ambitions, it is ultimately God's purpose that prevails. His plans are not like human plans, which can be flawed, uncertain, and subject to change. Instead, God's purposes are predestined, meaning they are established by His sovereign will and cannot be altered by the whims of time, circumstance, or human decision. This truth is both humbling and reassuring because it reminds us that we are part of something much greater than ourselves—an eternal, unchanging plan that reflects God's perfect wisdom and infinite love.

To fully appreciate the significance of God's predestined purpose, we must first understand the nature of predestination in the context of God's sovereignty. God's predestined purpose is like the foundation of a mighty fortress—solid, immovable, and unshakable. It stands firm no matter how the winds of change may blow or how the storms of life may rage. This is a truth that brings immense comfort and peace, especially in a world where so much seems uncertain and out of our control.

When we reflect on the reality that God's purpose is predestined, we are reminded that our lives are not random or meaningless. We are not drifting aimlessly through life, subject to the whims of fate or chance. Instead, we are part of a grand, divine plan that was set in motion by God Himself. This plan is not arbitrary or impersonal; it is filled with meaning, purpose, and intentionality. Every aspect of our lives—our joys and sorrows, our successes and failures, our relationships and experiences—is intricately woven into God's purpose. Nothing is wasted, and nothing is beyond God's control. This is a truth that can anchor our souls in the midst of life's uncertainties. When we face challenges or setbacks, when our plans fail or our dreams are shattered, we can take comfort in knowing that God's purpose still stands. His counsel will prevail, and His will is perfect.

One of the most comforting aspects of God's predestined purpose is that it is grounded in His unchanging character. God is not like humans, who can be fickle, unreliable, or swayed by circumstances. He is faithful, just, and true, and His purposes reflect these attributes. Because God is unchanging, His purposes are also unchanging. They are not subject to revision or alteration based on human actions or decisions. This means that no matter what happens in our lives or in the world around us, we can trust that God's purpose will be fulfilled. This trust is not based on wishful thinking or blind faith; it is rooted in the very nature of God, who is sovereign over all creation and who holds all things in His hands.

Living in alignment with God's predestined purpose means recognizing that our lives are part of His greater plan and seeking to align our will with His. It means submitting our desires, plans, and ambitions to Him, trusting that His purpose is better and wiser than anything we could ever conceive on our own. This is not always easy, especially when our plans seem good or when we face disappointment and loss. But it is in these moments that we are called to trust in God's sovereignty and to surrender to His will. This surrender is not an act of defeat, but of faith. It is a recognition that God's wisdom far surpasses our own and that His plans are always for our good.

Pursuing alignment with God's purpose also means seeking His guidance in all things. It means praying for wisdom and discernment, studying His Word to understand His will, and listening to the promptings of the Holy Spirit. It means being willing to let go of our own plans when they conflict with God's and being open to the new directions He may lead us. This requires humility, patience, and a willingness to trust in God's timing, even when it doesn't align with our own. But as we seek to align our lives with God's purpose, we will find that His plans are always better, richer, and more fulfilling than anything we could have imagined.

Another important aspect of living in alignment with God's predestined purpose is the peace and confidence it brings. When we trust in God's purpose, we are freed from the anxiety and worry that come from trying to control our own lives. We can rest in the assurance that God is in control and that His plans for us are good. This doesn't mean that life will always be easy or that we won't face difficulties, but it does mean that we can face those difficulties with a sense of peace and confidence, knowing that God's purpose will prevail. This trust in God's purpose allows us to live with a sense of freedom and joy, knowing that we are part of something much greater than ourselves.

God's predestined purpose also calls us to live with a sense of eternal perspective. It reminds us that our lives are not just about the here and now, but about something much bigger and more enduring. God's purpose is eternal, and it encompasses not just our individual lives, but all of history and all of creation. When we live with this eternal perspective, we are able to see our lives in the context of God's greater plan. We are able to focus on what truly matters, and we are less likely to be distracted or discouraged by the temporary trials and tribulations of this world. This eternal perspective gives us the strength to continue, the courage to face challenges, and the hope to keep moving forward, even when the way is difficult.

In practical terms, aligning our lives with God's predestined purpose means making decisions that reflect our trust in His plan. It means seeking His guidance in our choices, whether they are big or small, and being willing to follow where He leads, even when it's not what we expected or wanted. It means living with integrity, honoring God in our actions, our words, and our relationships. It means being faithful in the tasks and responsibilities He has given us, knowing that they are part of His greater purpose. And it means living with a sense of gratitude and contentment, trusting that God's plan for us is good, and that He is working all things together for our good.

One of the most powerful ways that God's predestined purpose impacts our lives is through the hope it gives us. When we understand that our lives are part of God's eternal plan, we are filled with a sense of purpose and meaning. We know that our lives have value and significance, not because of what we do or achieve, but because we are part of God's plan. This hope gives us the strength to keep going, even when life is hard, and the courage to face the future with confidence, knowing that God's purpose will prevail.

God's predestined purpose also calls us to live with a sense of mission. It reminds us that we are not here by accident, but that we have been placed in this time and place for a reason. God has a purpose for our lives, and He has given us gifts, talents, and opportunities to fulfill that purpose. This sense of mission gives us a sense of direction and focus, helping us to live intentionally and purposefully. It motivates us to use our gifts and talents for God's glory, to serve others, and to make a difference in the world. It reminds us that our lives are part of something much bigger than ourselves, and that we have a role to play in God's plan.

In conclusion, God's predestined purpose is a truth that brings deep comfort, peace, and hope to our lives. It is a reminder that our lives are not random or meaningless, but part of a grand, divine plan that is filled with purpose and meaning. God's purpose is unchanging and unalterable, grounded in His perfect wisdom and infinite love. As we seek to align our lives with His purpose, we are called to trust in His plan, to submit our will to His, and to live with a sense of eternal perspective and mission. In doing so, we will find the strength, courage, and hope we need to navigate life's challenges, knowing that God's purpose will prevail and that His plans for us are good. May we always pursue alignment with God's eternal purpose, trusting that His will is perfect and unchanging, and that our lives are part of His glorious, unshakable plan.

Chapter 8 - God's Perfect

God's perfect justice is like a solid, unyielding rock, providing a foundation of truth and righteousness that stands unshaken in a world often marred by unfairness, corruption, and injustice. In Deuteronomy 32:4, we are given a glimpse into the nature of God's justice: "He is the Rock, his work is perfect: for all his ways are judgment: a God of truth and without iniquity, just and right is he." These words reveal the essence of God's character—He is not only just, but His justice is perfect, flawless, and unchanging. Unlike human justice, which can be flawed, biased, or influenced by imperfect knowledge and motives, God's justice is pure and absolute. It is rooted in His perfect wisdom, His unerring truth, and His unchanging righteousness. This truth is deeply reassuring, especially when we see so much injustice in the world around us. When we encounter situations where wrong seems to prevail over right, where the innocent suffer and the guilty go free, it is comforting to know that God's justice will ultimately prevail. His ways are perfect, and His judgments are true; He sees all, knows all, and will one day set all things right.

To fully grasp the significance of God's perfect justice, we must first understand what it means for justice to be perfect. In human terms, justice often means giving each person what they deserve—punishing the guilty and protecting the innocent. But human justice is limited; it is often influenced by incomplete information, personal biases, or the limitations of human understanding. Even the best human judges can make mistakes or be swayed by factors that should not affect their decisions. But God's justice is different. It is not limited by time, perspective, or knowledge. God sees the whole picture—He knows every thought, every motive, every action, and every consequence. His justice is not only fair; it is perfect because it is administered by a God who is all-knowing, all-powerful, and perfectly holy.

God's perfect justice means that He will judge all things rightly, without partiality or favoritism. This is a truth that brings great comfort to those who have been wronged or who have suffered injustice. It means that no wrong will go unnoticed, no evil will go unpunished, and no good deed will go unrewarded. In a world where justice can often seem elusive, where the powerful can sometimes escape the consequences of their actions and the weak can be trampled underfoot, God's justice stands as a beacon of hope and assurance. It reminds us that there is a higher standard, a perfect judge who will one day bring true justice to every situation.

But God's justice is not only about punishment; it is also about restoration and redemption. In His perfect justice, God not only punishes sin but also provides a way for sinners to be redeemed. This is where God's justice intersects with His mercy. In His great love for us, God sent His Son, Jesus Christ, to take the punishment that we deserve so that we could be forgiven and restored to a right relationship with Him. This is the ultimate expression of God's perfect justice—He remains true to His nature as a just and holy God, while also extending grace and mercy to those who repent and turn to Him. Through Jesus, God's justice is satisfied, and His mercy is poured out on all who believe.

Living in light of God's perfect justice means pursuing a righteous life, knowing that we are accountable to a holy and just God. It means striving to live in a way that reflects God's character, seeking to do what is right and just in all our actions, words, and decisions. This is not about earning God's favor, but about responding to His grace with a heart that desires to please Him. It means being honest, fair, and compassionate in our dealings with others, knowing that God's justice requires us to act justly and love mercy. It also means standing up for those who are oppressed or treated unjustly, using our voices and our influence to advocate for what is right, knowing that God's heart is for justice and righteousness.

Trusting in God's perfect justice also means that we can let go of the need for personal revenge or retribution. When we are wronged, it is natural to want to take matters into our own hands, to seek to right the wrongs done to us. But God calls us to trust in His justice, to leave room for His judgment, knowing that He will repay every wrong and vindicate every injustice. This trust in God's justice frees us from the burden of carrying bitterness or hatred in our hearts. It allows us to forgive those who have wronged us, not because they deserve it, but because we trust that God will deal with them in His perfect time and way. This is not easy, but it is liberating, allowing us to live in peace and freedom, knowing that God's justice will prevail.

God's perfect justice also calls us to examine our own hearts and lives. It reminds us that we, too, are accountable to God for our actions and decisions. It is easy to focus on the injustices done to us or to others, but God's justice requires us to look inward as well. Are we living in a way that honors God's justice? Are we treating others fairly, with the respect and dignity they deserve as image-bearers of God? Are we standing up for what is right, even when it is difficult or unpopular? Are we seeking to reflect God's justice in our own lives, in the way we interact with others, in the decisions we make, and in the causes we support? These are challenging questions, but they are essential if we are to live in a way that honors God's perfect justice.

One of the most powerful aspects of God's perfect justice is that it gives us hope for the future. In a world that often seems unjust, where evil sometimes appears to have the upper hand, the promise of God's justice is a source of great hope and encouragement. We know that this world is not all there is, and that one day, God will set all things right. Every wrong will be righted, every injustice will be addressed, and God's perfect justice will prevail. This hope allows us to endure hardships, to persevere in the face of injustice, and to continue doing good, even when it seems like evil is winning. We can live with the assurance that God's justice will have the final word, and that in the end, righteousness and truth will triumph.

In practical terms, living in the light of God's perfect justice means being proactive in seeking justice in our world. It means not turning a blind eye to injustice, but actively working to bring about justice in our communities, our nations, and our world. This might mean advocating for those who are oppressed, standing up against systems of injustice, or simply being a voice for truth and righteousness in our everyday lives. It also means living with integrity, being honest in our dealings, and treating others with fairness and respect. It means being people who reflect God's justice in the way we live, the way we treat others, and the way we engage with the world around us.

God's perfect justice also provides us with a sense of security and peace. We live in a world where justice is often imperfect, where the guilty sometimes go unpunished and the innocent suffer. This can be deeply unsettling and can lead to feelings of fear, anger, or despair. But when we trust in God's perfect justice, we can rest in the assurance that ultimately, justice will be done. We can live with the confidence that God sees all, knows all, and will bring about justice in His perfect time and way. This doesn't mean that we are passive in the face of injustice, but that we are able to act with courage and conviction, knowing that we are on the side of a God who is just and right in all His ways.

In summary, God's perfect justice is a foundational truth that provides us with hope, comfort, and direction in our lives. It reminds us that we serve a God who is just, who judges rightly, and who will ultimately set all things right. His justice is perfect, immutable, and rooted in His unchanging character. As we live in the light of this truth, we are called to pursue a righteous life, to seek justice in our world, and to trust in God's perfect judgment. We are called to reflect His justice in our actions, our decisions, and our relationships, living with integrity, honesty, and compassion. And we are called to rest in the assurance that God's justice will prevail, that every wrong will be righted, and that in the end, righteousness and truth will triumph. May we always live in the light of God's perfect justice, trusting in His righteous judgment and seeking to reflect His justice in our lives and in our world.

Chapter 9 - God's Perpetual Peace

God's perpetual peace is like a tranquil river that flows steadily and unceasingly through the landscape of our lives, bringing calm, comfort, and serenity even in the midst of life's most chaotic storms. In Isaiah 26:3-4, we are given a powerful promise: "Thou wilt keep him in perfect peace, whose mind is stayed on thee: because he trusteth in thee. Trust ye in the LORD for ever: for in the LORD JEHOVAH is everlasting strength." These words offer us a glimpse into the depth and constancy of the peace that God provides—a peace that is not fleeting or dependent on our circumstances, but one that is eternal, unwavering, and deeply rooted in God's unchanging nature. God's peace is described as perfect, meaning it is complete, whole, and lacking nothing. It is a peace that transcends understanding, a peace that guards our hearts and minds even when everything around us seems to be falling apart. This peace is not something we can manufacture on our own; it is a gift from God, a reflection of His steadfast love and faithfulness toward us. It is a peace that anchors our souls, giving us the strength and stability we need to navigate the challenges of life with grace and confidence.

To truly understand the significance of God's perpetual peace, we must first reflect on what it means for peace to be perpetual. In human terms, peace is often seen as the absence of conflict or trouble, a temporary reprieve from the stresses and anxieties of life. But God's peace is different. It is not just a momentary escape from our problems; it is a continuous state of being that is available to us at all times, regardless of our circumstances. God's peace is perpetual because it is grounded in His eternal nature. Just as God does not change, His peace does not waver or diminish. It is a peace that is always present, always available, and always sufficient to meet our needs. This truth is deeply reassuring, especially in a world where so much is uncertain and where peace often seems elusive. When we are overwhelmed by the pressures of life, when we are faced with uncertainty or fear, we can find solace in the knowledge that God's peace is always there, like a steady current that carries us through the roughest waters.

One of the most beautiful aspects of God's perpetual peace is that it is not dependent on our external circumstances. In the world, peace is often linked to our situations—when things are going well, we feel at peace, but when challenges arise, our peace quickly evaporates. But God's peace is different. It is not based on what is happening around us, but on who God is. It is a peace that comes from trusting in God's character, His promises, and His sovereignty. When our minds are stayed on God, when we focus on His unchanging nature and His faithful love, we are kept in perfect peace, regardless of what is happening around us. This is a peace that is not shaken by the storms of life, a peace that remains steady even in the face of trials and tribulations. It is a peace that is rooted in the assurance that God is in control, that He is working all things together for our good, and that His plans for us are good.

Living in the light of God's perpetual peace means cultivating a mindset that is focused on God. It means choosing to keep our thoughts fixed on His truth, His promises, and His goodness, rather than being consumed by the worries and anxieties of life. This is not always easy, especially when we are faced with difficult situations or when the future seems uncertain. But it is in these moments that we are called to trust in God's peace, to rest in the knowledge that He is with us, and to allow His peace to guard our hearts and minds. This requires intentionality and discipline, a conscious effort to turn our thoughts toward God and to meditate on His Word. It means taking captive every thought that would steal our peace and replacing it with the truth of God's promises. As we do this, we begin to experience the fullness of God's peace, a peace that fills our hearts and minds and that permeates every aspect of our lives.

God's perpetual peace is also a source of strength and resilience. When we are at peace, we are better able to face the challenges of life with courage and confidence. We are not easily shaken by the difficulties we encounter, because we know that our peace is not dependent on our circumstances, but on God's unchanging nature. This peace gives us the strength to persevere, to keep moving forward even when the way is hard, and to trust that God is with us every step of the way. It is a peace that empowers us to live boldly, to take risks, and to pursue God's purpose for our lives, knowing that we are held securely in His hands.

Another important aspect of God's perpetual peace is that it is contagious. When we are living in God's peace, it spills over into our relationships and our interactions with others. We become instruments of God's peace, bringing calm, comfort, and reassurance to those around us. Our peaceful demeanor can have a powerful impact on others, helping to diffuse tension, ease anxiety, and bring healing to broken relationships. As we live in the light of God's peace, we become channels of that peace to the world around us, reflecting God's love and grace to those who are struggling or in need. This is one of the ways that we can be a light in the darkness, shining the light of God's peace into a world that is often filled with turmoil and unrest.

Living in God's perpetual peace also means being anchored in His promises. It means trusting that God is who He says He is, that He will do what He has promised, and that His plans for us are good. This trust is the foundation of our peace, the bedrock upon which our lives are built. When we trust in God, we are able to let go of our fears and anxieties, knowing that He is in control and that He will take care of us. This trust allows us to live with a sense of calm and assurance, even in the midst of life's challenges. It frees us from the need to worry about the future, to fret over things we cannot control, and to strive anxiously for security and stability. Instead, we are able to rest in the knowledge that God is our refuge, our fortress, and our ever-present help in times of trouble.

God's perpetual peace also invites us to live with an eternal perspective. It reminds us that this world is not all there is, and that our ultimate peace and security are found in God alone. When we focus on the eternal, we are able to see our present circumstances in a new light. We are less likely to be overwhelmed by the temporary trials and tribulations of this life, because we know that they are just that—temporary. Our hearts are anchored in the hope of eternity, and this gives us the strength to endure, to persevere, and to keep our eyes fixed on the prize that awaits us. This eternal perspective brings a deep sense of peace, knowing that no matter what happens in this life, our future is secure in God's hands.

In practical terms, living in God's perpetual peace means making choices that foster peace in our lives. It means being mindful of what we allow into our minds and hearts—what we watch, what we listen to, and what we meditate on. It means choosing to surround ourselves with people and influences that encourage peace, rather than those that stir up anxiety or unrest. It means setting aside time to be still, to pray, and to meditate on God's Word, allowing His peace to fill our hearts and minds. It also means being intentional about fostering peace in our relationships—seeking reconciliation, extending forgiveness, and being peacemakers in our interactions with others. As we do these things, we create an environment in which God's peace can thrive, both in our own lives and in the lives of those around us.

One of the most powerful ways that God's perpetual peace impacts our lives is through the way it transforms our outlook on life. When we are living in God's peace, we are able to see the world through a different lens. We are not easily swayed by the ups and downs of life, because our peace is not dependent on our circumstances, but on God's unchanging nature. This peace gives us a sense of stability and security, allowing us to face life's challenges with confidence and grace. It enables us to live with joy and contentment, even in the midst of difficulty, because we know that God is with us and that His peace is always available to us.

God's perpetual peace also calls us to be peacemakers in the world. It challenges us to be agents of peace in our families, our communities, and our world. This means being people who seek to resolve conflict, who bring healing to broken relationships, and who work for justice and reconciliation in the world. It means being people who embody God's peace in our actions, our words, and our attitudes, reflecting His love and grace to those around us. As we live in the light of God's peace, we become a powerful witness to the world of the peace that is available through a relationship with God.

In summary, God's perpetual peace is a truth that brings deep comfort, strength, and hope to our lives. It is a peace that is unwavering, eternal, and rooted in God's unchanging nature. As we live in the light of this truth, we are called to preserve a peaceful heart by keeping our minds focused on God, trusting in His promises, and resting in His love. We are called to be peacemakers in the world, reflecting God's peace to those around us, and living with an eternal perspective that gives us the strength to endure and the hope to persevere. May we always live in the light of God's perpetual peace, allowing it to fill our hearts and minds, and to guide our lives in every situation.

Chapter 10 - God's Permanent Salvation

God's permanent salvation is like an unshakable fortress that stands strong and secure throughout all of eternity, providing a place of refuge, peace, and unending hope in a world that is constantly changing and often filled with uncertainty. In Isaiah 51:6, the Bible offers us a profound and comforting truth: "Lift up your eyes to the heavens, and look upon the earth beneath: for the heavens shall vanish away like smoke, and the earth shall wax old like a garment, and they that dwell therein shall die in like manner: but my salvation shall be for ever, and my righteousness shall not be abolished." This verse paints a vivid picture of the impermanence of the physical world around us—the heavens will disappear like smoke, the earth will wear out like an old garment, and every living thing on it will eventually pass away. But in stark contrast to this fleeting nature of all that we see and know, God's salvation is described as eternal, unchanging, and forever secure. It is a salvation that is not subject to the wear and tear of time, not vulnerable to the decay that affects all earthly things, and not at risk of being altered or undone. It is a salvation that endures, a salvation that is rooted in God's immutable righteousness, and a salvation that provides us with the deepest assurance that we are safe and secure in His hands forever.

To fully grasp the depth and significance of God's permanent salvation, we must first reflect on the nature of salvation itself. Salvation, in its most profound sense, is the deliverance from sin, death, and eternal separation from God. It is the greatest gift that God has given to humanity, made possible through the life, death, and resurrection of Jesus Christ. Through His sacrifice, Jesus took upon Himself the penalty for our sins, offering us forgiveness, redemption, and the promise of eternal life with God. This salvation is not something we can earn or achieve on our own; it is a gift of grace, freely given by God to all who believe in Him. And because it is rooted in God's righteousness—His perfect, unchanging, and holy nature—it is a salvation that is as secure as God Himself. This is what makes God's salvation permanent: it is not dependent on us, on our actions, or on the changing circumstances of life; it is wholly dependent on God, who is the same yesterday, today, and forever.

This truth is both incredibly comforting and deeply empowering. It is comforting because it means that we do not have to live in fear of losing our salvation. We do not have to worry that our mistakes, our failures, or our shortcomings will somehow separate us from God's love or undo the work that Christ has done on our behalf. God's salvation is not something that can be taken away from us, not something that can be lost or forfeited. It is a permanent, unbreakable bond between us and God, secured by His promise and His righteousness. This assurance allows us to live with a sense of peace and confidence, knowing that our relationship with God is secure, that our future is certain, and that nothing can separate us from the love of God that is in Christ Jesus our Lord (Romans 8:38-39).

But God's permanent salvation is also empowering because it gives us the freedom to live boldly and joyfully in the present, knowing that our eternal destiny is secure. We are not bound by fear or anxiety about the future; instead, we can focus on living out our faith, loving others, and serving God with all our hearts, knowing that our salvation is secure. This security in our salvation allows us to face life's challenges with courage and resilience. We know that no matter what happens in this life—no matter how difficult our circumstances, how great our trials, or how deep our pain—God's salvation remains. It is the anchor for our souls, the solid rock on which we stand, and the source of our hope and joy, even in the midst of life's storms.

Living in the light of God's permanent salvation means placing our trust fully in Him and resting in the assurance of His promises. It means recognizing that our salvation is not based on our performance or our ability to live a perfect life, but on the finished work of Christ on the cross. It means embracing the truth that we are saved by grace through faith, not by works, so that no one can boast (Ephesians 2:8-9). This truth frees us from the burden of trying to earn God's favor or secure our own salvation; instead, we can rest in the knowledge that our salvation is a gift from God, given freely and securely, and that it is ours forever.

God's permanent salvation also calls us to live with a sense of gratitude and humility. When we truly understand the magnitude of what God has done for us—saving us from sin and death, giving us eternal life, and securing our place with Him forever—it fills our hearts with gratitude and compels us to live in a way that honors Him. This means living a life of obedience, not out of fear or obligation, but out of love and thankfulness for what God has done. It means seeking to grow in our relationship with God, to know Him more deeply, and to live in a way that reflects His love and grace to others. It also means being willing to share the good news of God's salvation with those who have not yet experienced it, so that they too can know the joy, peace, and security that comes from being saved by God.

One of the most beautiful aspects of God's permanent salvation is the peace that it brings to our hearts and minds. In a world that is often filled with uncertainty, where so much is temporary and transient, the assurance of God's eternal salvation provides a deep and abiding peace that nothing else can offer. It is a peace that comes from knowing that our lives are in God's hands, that our future is secure, and that we are loved and cherished by the Creator of the universe. This peace is not dependent on our circumstances; it is a peace that transcends understanding, a peace that guards our hearts and minds in Christ Jesus (Philippians 4:7). It is a peace that allows us to face life's challenges with calm and confidence, knowing that God is with us, that He is for us, and that our salvation is secure in Him.

Living in the assurance of God's permanent salvation also gives us a sense of purpose and direction. When we know that our salvation is secure, we are free to live out our calling with confidence and passion, knowing that our lives have eternal significance. We are no longer bound by the fear of failure or the need to prove ourselves; instead, we can focus on loving others, serving God, and making a difference in the world. This sense of purpose is grounded in the knowledge that we are part of God's eternal plan, that He has a purpose for our lives, and that He is using us to accomplish His will. This gives us the motivation to live with intentionality and to pursue the things that matter most—loving God, loving others, and living in a way that honors Him.

God's permanent salvation also provides us with hope, especially in the face of suffering and loss. When we experience pain, disappointment, or heartache, the assurance of God's eternal salvation gives us the strength to persevere, knowing that our suffering is temporary and that our future is secure. This hope is not just a wishful thinking; it is a confident expectation based on the promises of God, who cannot lie and who has promised us eternal life (Titus 1:2). This hope allows us to endure trials with patience and courage, knowing that God is with us, that He is working all things together for our good, and that one day, we will experience the fullness of His salvation in eternity.

In practical terms, living in the light of God's permanent salvation means making decisions that reflect our trust in God and our confidence in His promises. It means choosing to live in a way that honors God, knowing that our lives are part of His eternal plan. It means seeking to grow in our relationship with God, to know Him more deeply, and to live in a way that reflects His love and grace to others. It also means being willing to share the good news of God's salvation with those who have not yet experienced it, so that they too can know the joy, peace, and security that comes from being saved by God.

God's permanent salvation also invites us to live with an eternal perspective. It reminds us that this world is not our home, and that our ultimate hope and security are found in God alone. When we focus on the eternal, we are able to see our present circumstances in a new light. We are less likely to be overwhelmed by the temporary trials and tribulations of this life because we know that they are just that—temporary. Our hearts are anchored in the hope of eternity, and this gives us the strength to endure, to persevere, and to keep our eyes fixed on the prize that awaits us. This eternal perspective brings a deep sense of peace, knowing that no matter what happens in this life, our future is secure in God's hands.

In conclusion, God's permanent salvation is a truth that brings deep comfort, peace, and hope to our lives. It is a salvation that is secure, unchanging, and rooted in God's immutable righteousness. As we live in the light of this truth, we are called to place our rest in the eternal security of our salvation, knowing that it is rooted in God's unchanging character. We are called to live with a sense of gratitude and humility, to pursue our calling with confidence and passion, and to share the good news of God's salvation with others. And we are called to live with an eternal perspective, knowing that our ultimate hope and security are found in God alone. May we always rest in the assurance of God's permanent salvation, allowing it to fill our hearts with peace, our lives with purpose, and our souls with hope.

Chapter 11 - God's Perpetual Power

God's perpetual power is like a mighty force that has no beginning and no end, stretching across the vast expanse of eternity and holding all of creation together with unyielding strength and unwavering authority. In Psalm 90:2, we are reminded of this profound truth: "Before the mountains were brought forth, or ever thou hadst formed the earth and the world, even from everlasting to everlasting, thou art God." These words paint a picture of a God who is not only eternal but whose power is infinite and undiminished, a power that existed before the foundations of the world were laid and that will continue to reign supreme long after the earth and heavens have passed away. This truth is a source of deep comfort and awe because it tells us that the same God who created the universe with a word, who carved the mountains and spread out the seas, is the same God who holds our lives in His hands, guiding us, sustaining us, and providing for us with a power that never fades and never weakens. God's power is not like human strength, which can falter and fail; it is an everlasting, inexhaustible force that is always at work, always available, and always sufficient for every need.

To fully understand the significance of God's perpetual power, we must first grasp what it means for power to be perpetual. In human terms, power is often seen as something that can be gained or lost, something that ebbs and flows with time, circumstances, and human effort. But God's power is different. It is not something that fluctuates or diminishes; it is eternal, unchanging, and boundless. From the dawn of time, before the universe existed, God's power was already present, fully intact, and fully operational. This is a power that knows no limits, no exhaustion, and no decay. It is a power that sustains the stars in the sky, that keeps the earth spinning on its axis, and that holds every atom of creation together. And it is a power that is intimately involved in our lives, working in us and through us, guiding our steps, and providing for our every need.

This truth is incredibly comforting, especially when we face situations that seem overwhelming or impossible. In our human experience, we often encounter challenges that feel too big for us to handle, problems that seem insurmountable, and circumstances that leave us feeling powerless and afraid. But in those moments, we can take refuge in the knowledge that God's power is perpetual and undiminished. He is not limited by the same constraints that we are; His power is infinite, and it is always at work on our behalf. This means that no matter what we are facing, no matter how big the problem or how difficult the challenge, God's power is more than enough to see us through. We do not have to rely on our own strength or abilities; we can place our trust in God's omnipotence, knowing that His power is always available to sustain us, guide us, and carry us through whatever we may face.

Living in the light of God's perpetual power means embracing a mindset of trust and confidence in God's ability to work in our lives. It means recognizing that we are not alone in our struggles, that we do not have to carry our burdens on our own, and that we do not have to rely on our limited human strength to get by. Instead, we can lean on God's infinite power, knowing that He is always with us, always for us, and always able to meet our needs. This trust is not based on wishful thinking or blind faith; it is rooted in the very nature of God, who is all-powerful, all-knowing, and ever-present. When we trust in God's power, we are acknowledging that He is greater than any problem we could ever face, that He is in control of every situation, and that His power is more than sufficient to accomplish His purposes in our lives.

God's perpetual power is also a source of strength and encouragement when we feel weak or inadequate. In our human experience, it is natural to feel overwhelmed by the demands of life, to feel like we are not enough, or to struggle with feelings of inadequacy or fear. But when we understand that God's power is always at work within us, we are reminded that we are not relying on our own strength, but on the strength of the Almighty. This gives us the courage to face challenges, to step out in faith, and to pursue the things that God has called us to, knowing that we are not doing it alone. God's power is at work in us, enabling us to do things that we could never do on our own, giving us the strength to persevere, and providing us with the resources we need to fulfill our purpose.

Living in the light of God's perpetual power also means being aware of His presence in every aspect of our lives. God's power is not just something that is reserved for special occasions or big moments; it is something that is at work in the everyday, mundane details of our lives. It is the power that wakes us up in the morning, that gives us breath, that sustains us throughout the day, and that provides for our needs. It is the power that gives us the wisdom to make decisions, the courage to face challenges, and the strength to keep going when we feel like giving up. It is the power that comforts us in our pain, that gives us hope in our despair, and that fills us with peace in the midst of chaos. When we live with an awareness of God's perpetual power, we are able to see His hand at work in every aspect of our lives, guiding us, protecting us, and providing for us in ways that we may not even recognize.

God's perpetual power is also a source of hope and assurance for the future. In a world that is constantly changing, where so much is uncertain and where the future can often feel daunting or frightening, the knowledge that God's power is eternal and unchanging gives us a deep sense of security and peace. We do not have to fear the future because we know that God is already there, that His power is already at work, and that He is in control. This hope allows us to face the unknown with confidence, knowing that whatever the future holds, God's power will sustain us, guide us, and carry us through. It is a hope that is not based on our circumstances or our abilities, but on the unchanging nature of God, who is the same yesterday, today, and forever.

Living in the assurance of God's perpetual power also invites us to live with a sense of boldness and confidence. When we know that God's power is at work in us and through us, we are free to take risks, to step out in faith, and to pursue the things that God has placed on our hearts. We do not have to be held back by fear, doubt, or insecurity because we know that we are not doing it alone. God's power is with us, enabling us to do things that we could never do on our own, giving us the strength to overcome obstacles, and providing us with the resources we need to fulfill our purpose. This boldness is not about being reckless or arrogant; it is about having a deep and abiding trust in God's power and a willingness to follow where He leads, even when it is difficult or uncertain.

God's perpetual power also calls us to live with a sense of gratitude and humility. When we recognize that everything we have, everything we are, and everything we do is made possible by God's power, it fills our hearts with gratitude and compels us to live in a way that honors Him. It reminds us that we are not self-sufficient, that we are not in control, and that we are not the source of our own strength. Instead, we are dependent on God's power for everything, and this dependence is a beautiful and humbling reality. It leads us to a deeper appreciation of God's goodness and grace, and it motivates us to live in a way that reflects His love, His mercy, and His power to the world around us.

One of the most powerful aspects of God's perpetual power is the way it transforms our perspective on life's challenges. When we face difficulties, setbacks, or hardships, it is easy to feel overwhelmed or defeated. But when we understand that God's power is at work in us, we are reminded that we are not alone in our struggles. We have access to a power that is greater than anything we could ever imagine, a power that is more than sufficient to see us through whatever we may face. This understanding gives us the strength to persevere, the courage to keep going, and the hope to believe that things can and will get better. It allows us to face life's challenges with a sense of peace and assurance, knowing that God's power is always at work, always available, and always sufficient.

In practical terms, living in the light of God's perpetual power means making decisions that reflect our trust in His strength and our confidence in His ability to work in our lives. It means seeking God's guidance in all things, praying for His wisdom and strength, and being willing to step out in faith, even when it is difficult or uncertain. It means living with a sense of humility, recognizing that we are not the source of our own strength, and being willing to rely on God's power for everything. It also means living with a sense of gratitude and appreciation for all that God has done, and allowing His power to transform our lives and the lives of those around us.

God's perpetual power is also a source of inspiration and motivation for us to live lives that are bold, courageous, and full of faith. When we know that God's power is at work in us, we are free to pursue our dreams, to take risks, and to live with a sense of purpose and passion. We are not held back by fear, doubt, or insecurity because we know that we are not doing it alone. God's power is with us, enabling us to do things that we could never do on our own, giving us the strength to overcome obstacles, and providing us with the resources we need to fulfill our purpose. This inspiration is not about being reckless or arrogant; it is about having a deep and abiding trust in God's power and a willingness to follow where He leads, even when it is difficult or uncertain.

In conclusion, God's perpetual power is a truth that brings deep comfort, strength, and hope to our lives. It is a power that is eternal, unchanging, and boundless, a power that sustains the universe and holds our lives in His hands. As we live in the light of this truth, we are called to place our trust in God's omnipotence, knowing that His power is always at work, always available, and always sufficient for every need. We are called to live with a sense of gratitude and humility, recognizing that everything we have, everything we are, and everything we do is made possible by God's power. And we are called to live with a sense of boldness and confidence, knowing that God's power is at work in us, enabling us to do things that we could never do on our own, and providing us with the strength and resources we need to fulfill our purpose. May we always live in the light of God's perpetual power, allowing it to transform our lives and the lives of those around us, and trusting in His strength to guide us, sustain us, and carry us through whatever we may face.

Chapter 12 - God's Providential Guidance

God's providential guidance is like a steady hand on our shoulders, gently steering us through the complexities and uncertainties of life with a wisdom and care that is far beyond our understanding. In Psalm 32:8, God Himself speaks directly to us, saying, "I will instruct thee and teach thee in the way which thou shalt go: I will guide thee with mine eye." These words are not just a promise, but a profound declaration of God's unwavering commitment to lead us along the right path, no matter where we are or what we face. The idea that God, who created the heavens and the earth, would take such a personal interest in our individual lives is both humbling and awe-inspiring. His guidance is not like human advice, which can be fallible or limited; it is perfect, omniscient, and always directed toward our ultimate good. God's providential guidance means that He sees the big picture when we cannot, that He knows the best course for our lives even when we are confused or lost, and that He is actively involved in every step we take, ensuring that we are never truly alone in our journey.

To fully appreciate the depth and significance of God's providential guidance, we must first understand what it means for guidance to be providential. In human terms, guidance often means receiving advice or direction based on limited knowledge and perspective. But when we talk about God's guidance, we are talking about something infinitely greater. God's guidance is providential because it is rooted in His omniscience and sovereignty. He knows all things—past, present, and future—and He orchestrates the events of our lives in ways that are beyond our comprehension. He is not just a passive observer; He is actively involved in every detail of our lives, guiding us with precision and care. This means that nothing in our lives is random or accidental; everything is part of God's greater plan, designed to lead us toward the fulfillment of His purposes for us. Whether we are facing a major life decision, dealing with a difficult situation, or simply trying to find our way in a confusing world, we can trust that God's guidance is always perfect and always aligned with His will.

This truth is deeply comforting, especially when we find ourselves in situations where we feel uncertain or afraid. Life is full of decisions and challenges that can leave us feeling overwhelmed or unsure of which direction to take. In these moments, it is easy to feel lost or to doubt our ability to make the right choices. But God's promise in Psalm 32:8 reminds us that we are not navigating this life on our own. He is there with us, guiding us with His all-seeing eye, leading us down the path that He knows is best for us. This guidance is not just for the big decisions in life, but for every moment, every choice, and every step we take. God is intimately involved in our lives, and He is committed to leading us in the way that we should go. This means that we can have confidence, even in the face of uncertainty, because we know that God is in control and that His guidance is always reliable.

Living in the light of God's providential guidance means cultivating a heart of trust and dependence on Him. It means recognizing that our own understanding is limited and that we need God's wisdom and direction to navigate the complexities of life. This requires humility—a willingness to admit that we do not have all the answers and that we need God's help. It also requires faith—a belief that God is who He says He is and that He will do what He has promised. When we trust in God's guidance, we are acknowledging that He is the one who knows the way forward, that He sees what we cannot see, and that His plans for us are good. This trust allows us to let go of our fears and anxieties, knowing that God is leading us and that He will not let us stray from the path He has chosen for us.

God's providential guidance is also a source of strength and encouragement when we face challenges or difficulties. In life, we often encounter situations that are beyond our control, circumstances that leave us feeling powerless or overwhelmed. But when we trust in God's guidance, we are reminded that we are not alone in our struggles. God is with us, guiding us through the storm, leading us to safe harbor. His guidance is not just a map that shows us the way; it is a constant presence that walks with us every step of the journey. This means that even when we face obstacles or setbacks, we can have confidence that God is still in control and that He is leading us toward the fulfillment of His purposes. This confidence gives us the strength to persevere, to keep moving forward, and to trust that God is working all things together for our good.

Living in dependence on God's providential guidance also means being open to His leading in every aspect of our lives. It means seeking His guidance in prayer, asking for His wisdom, and being willing to follow where He leads, even when it is difficult or uncertain. It means being sensitive to the promptings of the Holy Spirit, listening for God's voice, and being willing to adjust our plans or change our direction when He calls us to do so. This requires a heart that is surrendered to God, a heart that is willing to put aside our own desires and ambitions in favor of God's will. But as we learn to trust in God's guidance, we will find that His way is always better, His plans are always wiser, and His purposes are always for our good.

God's providential guidance also calls us to live with a sense of peace and assurance. When we know that God is guiding us, we can rest in the confidence that we are on the right path, even when the way is difficult or unclear. This peace comes from knowing that God is in control, that He is leading us, and that His guidance is always for our good. It allows us to let go of our worries and anxieties, to trust that God is working out His purposes in our lives, and to live with a sense of calm and assurance, even in the midst of life's challenges. This peace is not something we can manufacture on our own; it is a gift from God, a reflection of His constant presence and His unwavering commitment to guide us.

God's providential guidance also invites us to live with a sense of purpose and direction. When we trust in God's guidance, we are not just wandering aimlessly through life; we are walking on a path that has been carefully chosen for us by the Creator of the universe. This gives our lives meaning and significance, knowing that we are part of God's greater plan and that He is leading us toward the fulfillment of His purposes. This sense of purpose motivates us to live intentionally, to make choices that honor God, and to pursue the things that He has called us to. It also gives us the courage to step out in faith, to take risks, and to follow God's leading, even when it takes us outside of our comfort zones.

In practical terms, living in dependence on God's providential guidance means making decisions that reflect our trust in His wisdom and direction. It means seeking God's guidance in prayer, asking for His wisdom and discernment, and being willing to follow where He leads, even when it is difficult or uncertain. It means living with a sense of humility, recognizing that we do not have all the answers, and being willing to submit our plans and desires to God's will. It also means living with a sense of peace and assurance, knowing that God is guiding us, that He is in control, and that His plans for us are good.

One of the most powerful ways that God's providential guidance impacts our lives is through the way it transforms our perspective on life's challenges. When we face difficulties, setbacks, or obstacles, it is easy to feel overwhelmed or discouraged. But when we trust in God's guidance, we are reminded that we are not alone in our struggles. God is with us, leading us through the storm, guiding us with His all-seeing eye, and working out His purposes in our lives. This understanding gives us the strength to persevere, the courage to keep moving forward, and the hope to believe that things can and will get better. It allows us to face life's challenges with a sense of peace and assurance, knowing that God's guidance is always perfect and that He is leading us toward the fulfillment of His purposes.

God's providential guidance also calls us to live with a sense of gratitude and humility. When we recognize that everything we have, everything we are, and everything we do is made possible by God's guidance, it fills our hearts with gratitude and compels us to live in a way that honors Him. It reminds us that we are not self-sufficient, that we are not in control, and that we need God's wisdom and direction to navigate the complexities of life. This dependence is a beautiful and humbling reality that leads us to a deeper appreciation of God's goodness and grace. It motivates us to live in a way that reflects His love, His mercy, and His guidance to the world around us.

In conclusion, God's providential guidance is a truth that brings deep comfort, strength, and hope to our lives. It is a guidance that is perfect, omniscient, and always directed toward our ultimate good. As we live in the light of this truth, we are called to depend on God's unchanging guidance, trusting that He will lead us in the right path at all times. We are called to live with a sense of humility, recognizing that we need God's wisdom and direction, and being willing to submit our plans and desires to His will. We are called to live with a sense of peace and assurance, knowing that God is guiding us, that He is in control, and that His plans for us are good. And we are called to live with a sense of purpose and direction, knowing that our lives have meaning and significance because we are walking on a path that has been carefully chosen for us by the Creator of the universe. May we always live in the light of God's providential guidance, allowing it to transform our lives and the lives of those around us, and trusting in His wisdom and direction to lead us in the way we should go.

Conclusion

As we draw to a close on our journey through "The Immutable Fortress: Security in God's Unchanging Nature," we find ourselves anchored in a profound truth that transcends the shifting sands of life. We have explored the depths of God's immutable character—His perpetual faithfulness, unwavering justice, and everlasting love. These attributes form an unbreakable fortress around us, a refuge where we can find peace, strength, and confidence no matter what challenges we face. In a world that is constantly changing, where uncertainty and fear often threaten to overwhelm us, the unchanging nature of God is our steadfast hope. It is the assurance that, no matter how turbulent our circumstances, we are held securely in the hands of a God who is the same yesterday, today, and forever.

As Christians, this truth is not just a comfort to cling to in times of trouble; it is a foundation upon which we are called to build our lives. The security we find in God's unchanging nature should propel us forward in our walk with Him, giving us the courage to face the unknown with faith and the resolve to live out our calling with purpose. Knowing that God's character is immutable should challenge us to deepen our trust in Him, to lean on His promises with unwavering confidence, and to pursue a life that reflects His steadfastness.

But this is not a passive journey. As we rest in the security of God's unchanging nature, we must also be active participants in our faith. We are called to continually seek His guidance, to immerse ourselves in His Word, and to allow His truth to transform us. This walk with the Lord is a daily commitment to align our lives with His will, to surrender our fears and doubts, and to trust that He is leading us along the path He has ordained. It is a challenge to live boldly, knowing that our foundation is firm and our hope is secure.

The unchanging nature of God is not only our comfort; it is our commission. As we stand firm in the fortress of His character, we are called to reflect His constancy to the world around us. In our relationships, in our decisions, and in the way we respond to life's challenges, we should strive to embody the same faithfulness, love, and justice that define our God. By doing so, we become living testimonies of the security found in Him, drawing others toward the refuge we have found.

In conclusion, the immutable nature of God is the bedrock of our faith and the source of our strength. It is the fortress that surrounds us, protecting us from the storms of life and providing us with unshakable security. But more than that, it is the foundation from which we are called to live boldly, to trust deeply, and to walk faithfully with the Lord. As we continue our journey, let us do so with the confidence that comes from knowing we are held by a God who never changes, whose love never fails, and whose promises are forever true.

Don't miss out!

Visit the website below and you can sign up to receive emails whenever Joshua Rhoades publishes a new book. There's no charge and no obligation.

https://books2read.com/r/B-A-AJLBB-FOHWE

Did you love *The Immutable Fortress- Security in God's Unchanging Nature*? Then you should read *Sounding The Call - The Voice of Conviction*[1] by Joshua Rhoades!

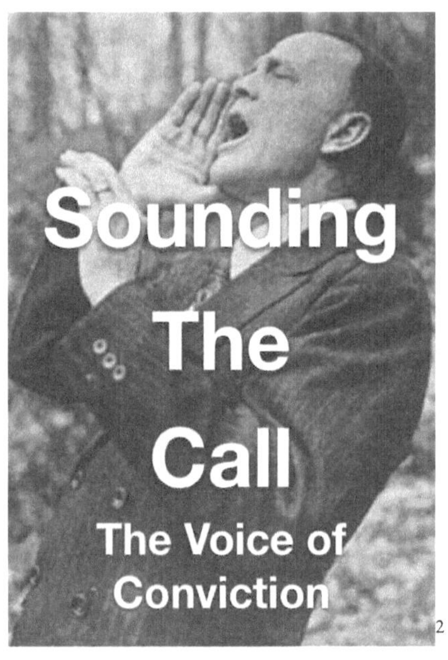

In a world filled with noise, where countless voices vie for our attention, the voice of conviction often stands out as a beacon of truth and clarity. This voice, rooted in the divine call to righteousness, echoes through the ages, urging humanity to confront sin, seek justice, and return to a life aligned with God's will. Isaiah 58:1 captures this urgency and powerfully encapsulates the role of the prophet: "Cry aloud, spare not, lift up thy voice like a trumpet, and shew my people their transgression, and the house of Jacob their sins." This verse is not merely a relic of ancient scripture but a timeless call that remains profoundly relevant today.

---

1. https://books2read.com/u/ba5XVy

2. https://books2read.com/u/ba5XVy

"Sounding The Call - The Voice of Conviction" is a deep exploration of Isaiah 58:1, its significance, and its pressing relevance for our contemporary world. This book looks into the heart of the prophet's mandate, examining the imperative to speak out against wrongdoing, to call out injustice, and to urge communities back to the path of righteousness. In an era where moral relativism often blurs the lines between right and wrong, the clarion call of Isaiah 58:1 reminds us of the unchanging standards of God's truth and the necessity of upholding them with courage and conviction.

Today, as in the days of Isaiah, the world is in desperate need of voices that are unafraid to speak the truth. The command to "cry aloud" is not just for the prophets of old; it is a charge to every believer to lift their voice against the injustices and sins that plague our societies. Whether it is addressing the deep-seated issues of inequality, corruption, or moral decay, the message of Isaiah 58:1 is a powerful reminder that silence is not an option when faced with evil. The call to "spare not" emphasizes the need for unwavering commitment to truth, even when it is inconvenient or unpopular. It challenges us to confront our own complacency and to take an active stand in the face of wrongdoing.

This book also explores the metaphor of the trumpet used in Isaiah 58:1—a symbol of urgency, clarity, and the need to capture attention. Just as a trumpet blast cuts through the noise, the voice of conviction must be bold and clear, leaving no room for ambiguity. In a time when many are reluctant to speak out for fear of criticism or backlash, "Sounding The Call" encourages readers to embrace their role as bearers of truth, to lift their voices without fear, and to stand firm in their convictions.

"Sounding The Call - The Voice of Conviction" is not just an exposition of Isaiah 58:1; it is a call to action. It invites readers to reflect on the relevance of this ancient text in their own lives and to consider how they can be voices of conviction in their communities. In exploring the need for prophetic voices today, this book challenges each of us to examine our own response to the injustices we see around us and to be willing to "cry aloud" in the pursuit of righteousness.

As you journey through these pages, may you be inspired to listen to the voice of conviction within you, to boldly proclaim the truth, and to live out the call of Isaiah 58:1 in a world that desperately needs it. The time to sound the call is now. The voice of conviction is yours to lift.